ENTERING THE DAY

ALSO BY
MICHAEL MILLER

The Joyful Dark
The Singing Inside
Darkening the Grass
Into This World
Lifelines
The Different War
In the Mirror
Asking the Names
Waking in the Dark

Entering the Day

POEMS

BY MICHAEL MILLER

PINYON PUBLISHING
Montrose, Colorado

Cover Art "Protea from the Upcountry Farmer's Market, Maui" by Susan Entsminger

Photograph of Michael Miller by Harlon Miller

First Edition: April 2020

Pinyon Publishing
23847 V66 Trail, Montrose, CO 81403
www.pinyon-publishing.com

Library of Congress Control Number: 2020930016
ISBN: 978-1-936671-63-2

ACKNOWLEDGMENTS

Some of these poems, in slightly different versions, appeared in:

Commonweal
Gemini Magazine
Passager
Pinyon Review
The Sewanee Review
Witness

for Nick Lyons

and to the memory of Mari Lyons

CONTENTS

I

II

III

IV

V

I

IN MY DREAMS

I need my dreams
To open the fist inside me,
To let out the rage, the loss,
An angry old man
Who could destroy
Instead of create.

In my dreams I meet
The women of kindness,
The gentle men, the nurturing
Strangers who lead me
Out of despair and into
The places of light.

Diminishments, deprivations,
The isolation I grapple with
Disappear as I awaken
At four in the morning
And the fist opens,
The hand reaches out.

ON NAUSET BEACH

Beyond my limitations of old age,
Lovemaking restricted
To positions without pain,
Footsteps balanced with
The aid of a trustworthy cane,
I stride through the surprise
Of a sunswept morning
On a shoulder of Nauset Beach
Singing to the Atlantic,
The thrashing incoming tide,
The waves breaking onto the shore
Like sleeves of ruffled lace,
The gannets swooping
With black-tipped wings
Beating a welcome
As my uncommon dream continues,
As I am one with the sea,
The sky, the enveloping world
That surrounds me, that lifts me
Out of the grinding jaws
That chew through my days,
Mutilate my nights.
I will keep this dream
In looping cursive,
In black ink on the white pages
Of my blue-lined notebook
Drawing me back to the boy
Who practiced his penmanship
With the innocence of first love.

I will describe everything
I have seen on Nauset Beach:
The hermit crabs inscribing
The sand, the pieces
Of green polished glass,
The chunk of driftwood
A castle for beetles and ants.
I will return to my beach
On every occasion
When dread visits my thoughts
And sleep is an elusive friend.

MORNING SONG IN AMHERST

Eight minutes from home,
Passing slender birches
With trunks of peeling bark,
Up a newly paved driveway
Where a horse-drawn carriage
Once clattered, I found someone
On my solitary seat.
"Look at me," said a moon-faced
Woman shaded with embarrassment
In her grime-streaked woolen coat
In July, her hair a tangled nest
No bird would return to
As she gazed up from
The maple bench
Beside the Dickinson home,
A cigarette between
Her dirty fingers.
Emily would have sat down,
Waited a long moment
Before asking her name
And offering a bath and breakfast;
All I could do was
Stand silently, listening
To a hermit thrush
Begin its morning song.
"Where's the birdy?" she asked,
Her watery eyes looking toward
A profusion of leaves.
"I slept here all night,
No one bothered me,"

And the great oak said nothing,
And the rectangular garden
In full bloom made no reply.
"I won't bother you," I said,
"But if you would like a bath
And breakfast come home with me,"
And I reached down
To help her up and almost heard
Emily say, "Yes, oh yes!"

SPEAKING WITH MY SON

After I put down the phone
I continue to speak.
Have you been fishing?
You tell me about your son
Casting in your beloved bayous,
His eyes brightening as he
Lifted a redfish, wriggling,
Then removed the hook by himself.
I never mention how you walked away
From your smashed blue pick-up
After the crash on the thruway.
I do not say God was watching
Or hear you say, "Fate."
Now it is time to say goodnight,
To turn off the lamp
And see you paddling past
A swamp magnolia with
Five white egrets poised
On long, curving branches.

PAST THE DUNES

No stars, no moon,
The long beams of our flashlights
Leading the way over the sand,
Past the dunes, the driftwood,
The spears of tall grass.
We stopped, turned off
The lights, listened.
An animal screamed,
Talons had struck.
We felt for each other's arm
As if we were blind,
As if we were the prey.

DELIRIUM

All those yesterdays in memory!
Your unblemished body,
Our lust a blue delirium
Through the nights of luminous joy
In our small apartment
As the radiator clanked into dawn.
Today, between the hills
Of Massachusetts,
I kiss your old age into sleep,
Into waking with birdsong.

MORNING IN REPOSE

Lying on your side
With the blanket drawn up
To your bare shoulder
You are the peacefulness
In the sunlight
That comes through the window,
Too beautiful to awaken
In these moments
That love and the decades
Have given. Once again
Old age surprises me
With its blessings.

CEREMONY

We need a ceremony
To celebrate our lasting love,
To ignore the forecast of death;
Death tomorrow,
Death after a decade.

For these long minutes
May my kisses restore our innocence—
The only ceremony I know
Begins with our arms
Around each other.

II

A DIFFERENT TIME

In my seventy-eighth spring
I dreamt of Jack,
The man I wanted to call Father,
The gray-haired Catholic
Who told me Jesus brought
Goodness into the world
But never walked on water,
Who loved Mother but could not
Divorce his wife,
Who left welts across my buttocks
Until I learned right from wrong,
The man whose blue sapphire ring
I wear today.
Jack landed in the first wave
On Iwo Jima,
The Marine on his right
Stitched with bullets
Across his chest.
In a different time
I trained in the jungle
On Okinawa, made landings
On the beaches.
He asked about the peacetime Corps,
Boot Camp at Parris Island
As we walked across
A meadow in Massachusetts
Far from the black sand
Of that island
Where he left his blood;
His Purple Heart remained in
The glove compartment of

His Buick beside his pistol.
He asked about my son,
My grandchildren,
My silver-haired wife.
He put his right hand
On my left shoulder
As I awakened
And that was everything.

TIDE OF BLOOD

His eyes close for a moment
And the unwanted thoughts return—
The waves of killing have changed
But death remains the same,
The tide of blood continuing,
Its steady flow still in his dreams,
Reddening the sand of Omaha Beach.
He remembers the lives deprived
Of their future, the letters
He was asked to mail, "In case,"
And with each whiskey and cigarette
Another comrade appears, his face
Still innocent across the table.

THE MEMORY

At breakfast he reads about ISIS,
Air strikes, and mutters, "Another war,"
Then finishes his stewed prunes,
Remembers the powdered eggs
He ate after Pork Chop Hill,
The dead bodies in the coffins of snow.
Washing the bowl, he wishes he could
Wash away the memories of Korea:
The man he killed, plunging his bayonet
Into his gut, the hand-to-hand combat,
The intimacy he lives with still.

SCARS

When he passes them on the forgiving field
A woman with a face as brown as earth smiles
And he sees the scar across her forehead
And wonders if she was struck by shrapnel
In the rice paddies of Vietnam
Where she and the other women lived
Before they found sanctuary between
The hills in Massachusetts.
They work twenty acres
Without planes dropping napalm
Or rifles stuttering
From the tapestry of trees.
They always wave to him
And probably never consider
How he once carried a rifle
Through the jungles of their country.
He would like to take off his shirt
And show them the scar on his back,
Then join them in the field
To work under the sun
In the slow dance of the wind.

RIFLEMAN'S EYE

Rolling onto his side,
Swinging his dead legs
Over the edge of the bed
He sits up, presses down
On the mattress with his fists
And lifts his body
Into the wheelchair.
This is how he begins his day,
Far from Iraq,
From roadside bombs
And missions through
The green world
Of night vision goggles.
Soon he will hear
The call of the warbler,
Scan the trees with
A rifleman's eye for
Its yellow feathers.
"Live," he says,
Gazing at the warbler,
Not at the vultures
Picking at body parts.

BETWEEN MISSIONS

Bobby Ray strummed his guitar,
The Afghani dirt alive
With men dancing
Who might be dead tomorrow.

Bare-chested and tattooed,
They moved with spontaneous steps,
In love with themselves
But ready to die for each other.

THIS RIFLE

Again and again he cleaned his rifle
Using a rag, a brush, a patch with oil,
Assuring himself the barrel, the trigger,
The Leupold scope were immaculate;
He could take it apart in the dark,
Put it together quickly.
This rifle was not his father's,
Not his decorated uncle's,
It was *his* rifle;
The stock a perfect fit against
His shoulder, the trigger made
For his finger. This rifle was
Marine Corps issue; it was not meant
For killing deer in the woods of Vermont.

KILLING

The squirrel hung from
His cat's clenched jaw,
Still trembling.

The cat brings it onto the porch,
Stands before him
Displaying his trophy.

Animals kill purely,
Driven by instinct far from
Designed murder.

Tell him, lieutenant,
Everything he didn't learn
At West Point.

The artistry of ambush,
Counterattack, crossfire,
It was never meant for a private.

He was taught to waste them,
Waste them one after another
Without a thought.

Vietnam was over,
Then came insurgents,
The Taliban.

Tell him, captain,
How careers are made,
How useful sergeants can be.

His rifle kept immaculate,
His guilt washed away
Like blood in the sink.

What will be next?
Constantly training,
He will always be ready.

Ready on the right,
Ready on the left,
All ready on the firing line!

Sights lined up,
Measure the range,
Breathe in, breathe out.

Squeeze the trigger,
Never pull it, jerk it,
Make the shot count.

One perfect shot,
One clean kill,
One head a poppy exploding.

Yes, major, we advanced,
The area is secure.
The casualties light.

Three Purple Hearts,
Two Bronze Stars,
One letter home.

This is his home,
Meant for his cat,
Not the dead squirrel.

He takes it to the woods,
Puts it beside his buried medals
But not his memories.

Milburn, Tuttle, Yardley,
Humping the hills
Before the explosion.

Shrapnel severing limbs—
Tighten the tourniquets,
Plug the holes.

Shooting the dogs
Scavenging for body pieces,
Killing them quickly.

His trigger finger a reflex,
His reason dislodged,
The carnage a monument.

He poured another round
For Milburn, Tuttle, Yardley,
Raising his glass.

If only this dream
Recurred, if only it would
Replace the nightmares.

Whiskey shortens the night,
Thrushes sing at daybreak.
He listens, he listens for his dead.

III

AN ISOLATED MAN, CONTINUING

"Isolation!" he shouts in his mind,
Pronouncing each syllable
Like a word in an unwelcome language
He has reluctantly begun to learn
As if he could dispel
His loneliness
On his morning walk
Past the brick station
Where no one arrives,
No one departs,
Where he continues
Past the pine grove
And cluster of sugar maples
Where no bird sings,
Where the fallen leaves
Curl into themselves
And dying might be
His last friend.
If only one crow would appear
To screech its soul
Into the day and assure him
Of the remaining life in winter
He might be able to settle
Into the bareness
And salvage a reason to live.
If only his ex-wife
In love with mirrors
And his self-centered
Estranged son would say
A kind word when he calls

He might begin to caress
His wounds and mistakes
That have never been
Forgotten, forgiven.
"Can I learn to live
With dying?" he asks,
Continuing his walk
Without a thought
Of turning back,
Of entering his empty house.
He stops, he reconsiders;
The sunlight on his back,
His shadow is on the wide
Oak tree before him,
He feels a part of all things.

THE WOUND

On the bus he sat
Beside her, her singular aura
Drawing him to her.
She smiled with a warmth
Absent from his life,
A man turning fifty
With a history of mistakes,
The wrong turnings
On the right road.
He needed to love again,
To heal the wound within
That had opened after years
As if the stitches
Had been removed too soon
And a small seepage
Of blood now appeared
On the sheet each morning.
Was she the healer,
The stranger
He had always needed?
They sat quietly
Waiting for the other
To speak.

AN ORDERLY MAN

He wears his life,
Washing it carefully,
Ironing it like his shirts
He places in the third drawer.
He goes out at sunrise,
Looks for secrets
In the trees,
The available leaves
Have nothing to tell.

CROSSING

Near the border the cacti
Stand like thorned sculpture,
Crossing guards patrol in jeeps,
Holstered pistols on their hips.

A rattlesnake coils, uncoils,
The day eases into night
As men, children,
And determined women arrive.

Now thwarted dreams
Belong to others, a language
Waits to be learned,
The uncertain future is real.

AN OLD WOMAN'S PASSION

An old woman's passion
Scorched the air
As she spoke about the injustice
She had witnessed
In her eighty-six years,
Its significance not changing
A sentence in the pages of history.
She would continue to speak,
Her rail-thin body, wrinkled face
And sharp words mesmerizing
Anyone who would listen.

REMEMBERING THE WORDS

Drinking her coffee she whispers,
"Starfish, violets, Alaska, hummingbird,"
Then closes her eyes, opens them
And repeats the words.
Ten minutes later, after reading
About the terrorist attack,
She tries to remember the words,
Testing herself for those signs
Leading to the land of bewilderment.
Delighted, she goes out,
Looking for the hummingbird.

PRESCRIPTION

The young woman doing T'ai Chi
On the common nodded when he waved.
He wished he could drop his cane,
Hurry across the grass to join her,
To do something new
Beyond his prescriptions for life.
He could only stand there,
His old body unable to bend
With her graceful movements.
But his unrestricted spirit
Moved with her arms and her legs
Through each precise gesture
Almost rising with her.

AGELESS

She can no longer bend
Over the sink
To wash the night away
And wets a napkin
To wipe her eyes with
A gentleness that reminds her
Of his fingers—
How he touched her
With undying tenderness
Through their gift of years.
At these moments he is
With her to begin the day
In her ninety-third spring,
His love in an ageless place
Nothing can disturb.

THE ADDRESS BOOK

In the small address book
He has the urge to draw
A line across the names
And phone numbers
Of his dead friends.
He will keep them alive
In his memory, in his cursive,
Evoke their images
When he reads their names.
Tomorrow he will add
His name, his wife
And daughter's name;
Yes, even his grandchildren—
The living and the dead,
All in their breathing addresses.

PERENNIALS

Lying as stiff as death,
Letting her thoughts dwell
On the past, letting them return
To their home in the present,
She wishes it was
The deep black forever.
Turning onto her side,
Shifting her weight
To lessen the pain,
She looks at the shape
Of the chair, the outline
Of the dresser,
The vase without a rose.
She moves her hand
Across the bed to
Where her husband slept,
The space evoking
His presence: his wit,
His laughter, how he could
Speak about anything
And make love without a word.
Now she lifts herself,
Rising into the emptiness
Of her days, her nights,
Her one great loss
The foundation of others.
She will rebuild her life,
She will fill it with
Trips to the city,
Classics to reread,
Caring for the rose bushes

She planted with her husband,
The clusters of orange,
White, and crimson lilies
In a corner of the garden;
She will prune, plant,
Rearrange the perennials
And wait for their blooms.
She will get through
Her seventy-third winter.
"Be strong," her husband said,
His last words.

THE OLD COUPLE

They can no longer
Make their bed alone;
They begin, one on each side
Pulling up the sheet perfectly.
Last night his left foot
Belonged to someone else;
He feels too old to see
A doctor about its numbness,
Something will kill him
Today or tomorrow.
He has lived a quiet life.
If death comes loudly
He will ignore it
But not the deep silence
Of his love for his wife
Who refuses a hearing aid,
A visit to the doctor.
"Do the trees get
A check-up?" she asks.
He answers with a kiss,
Always with a kiss
Instead of words.

FEEDER

With the hand-carved cane
That belonged to her husband
She walks through
The six yards of fresh snow
To the feeder by her house,
Her moon-white hair
Beneath her black hat.
"Food for my little ones,"
She murmurs, thinking of how
The birds fly into her life,
The birds she counts
Every day, listing them
In a letter to her husband,
Never sent.

EACH WEEK

Bedridden at ninety-five,
Her long white hair
Always combed,
She drifts in, she drifts out
Of that place
No one can reach.
She recognizes the flowers
He brings. "Daffodils," she says
At the beginning of spring,
"And who are you?"

A WOMAN IN WINTER

She wants clear light,
Not the nets of shadow
Cast by the three lamps
In her living room with
Old photographs on the bookcase
And memories never dusted.

She imagines the slow motion
Days of summer, her asters
And rose bushes blooming;
She has always found something
To lift her spirit
Into the garden of light.

FROM HEDGE TO HEMLOCK

Six yards from his bed
The recliner waits.
At five in the morning,
Awakened by a nightmare,
He rises and wobbles toward it,
A brittle tower of bones.
Stretching out his legs,
Bending each one five times,
Flexing his swollen fingers
Until he can close his hands,
He leans back, shuts his eyes
And imagines a purple finch
Perched on a telephone wire,
A yellow-throated warbler
On a maple's leafy branch,
The rare scarlet tanager
Darting from hedge to hemlock.
"I hope to see you," he says,
Eager for his walk at sunrise,
High point of his day
That fills him with gratitude
For his feathery songsters
Who will sing to him,
Their high-pitched notes
Piercing his loneliness,
Pushing aside his demon
That whispers, "Die, die
Old man, your life
Has no value now."
"You're wrong," he states,
Rising from the recliner.

"I'll be there soon,"
And he knows the chickadees
Will be at the fountain.

IV

VIRGINIA

There was no lighthouse in sight,
No beacon to brighten the night,
No Lytton asking for her hand,
No Leonard to sooth her multiple selves
And love her through madness,
No Vanessa, no Vita, her Orlando—
She was entirely alone, a prisoner
Of beginnings, of endings, with
Stones in her pockets, the River Ouse
Surrounding her, a dark skirt unfashionable.

She remembered the birds singing
In Greek, the plane trees with
Asymmetrical windows opened wide
Between their bare branches,
The secrets she looked for in
Her father's beard. And to the tightness
Of her mother's closed lips she whispered,
"Let me in," knowing her words
Were meant to be elsewhere,
In perfect sentences she could control.

AHAB

Let them call him mad;
What do they know of madness,
Its glorious shapes,
Its mysterious reach,
Its path halfway toward bedlam?
Call it a twist of soul,
A divergence from reason,
A single-minded pursuit
That drove him
Beyond the ordinary.
His crooked being was true
To the colossal sea,
The verandahs of waves,
The course of shifting tides
And his quest that others
Called obsessive.
"There she blows!"
Are Starbuck's words
That aroused his blood,
Fevered his brain.

For hours, for days
He paced the Pequod's deck,
Smoked his briarwood pipe,
Gazed into that unruly blue
And was mesmerized by
Its swells, its calms,
Until it rose toward
A tumultuous eruption
Encompassing the shark,
The dolphin, the humpbacked whale

But not his Moby Dick
Diving toward a shipwreck's skeleton.
Husband, wife, mistress,
His white whale contained all,
Keeping him alive
When all else failed,
Drawing him from
His land-locked life
That was predictable,
A muted cry
For voyages unending.

He should have been born
With fins, with the shark's
Sickle-shaped mouth
And double row
Of immaculate teeth.
He had never been content,
A man of limitations,
Of mind in permanent exile
From those high estates.
Give him an albatross's wings,
The sperm whale's tail.

Tonight he will sharpen
His harpoon, rub his thumb
Along its razor edge
As Queequeg does religiously,
Return to his quadrant,
Maps and charts,
Plot the course toward

Those inscrutable waters
Where Moby Dick waits,
Waiting for him
Or indifferent to him.

Soon the chase will begin,
"Lower the boats, Mr. Stubb!"
Soon he will be upon him,
Raise his harpoon
And plunge it into
His massive brain
That has outwitted him
For so long; he has
Become his nemesis
And singular love,
His curse, his blessing,
The salvation always
Beyond his grasp.

TOLSTOY DREAMING

His wife is stealing his dreams,
Taking them to a place beyond
His reach, breaking them down
To parts, selling them
With a refurbished ending
And reassembled beginning
To anyone in need.
He has no objections,
Perhaps his dreams were theirs.

She is always eating venison
In his recurring dream,
Cutting it into small pieces.
When she lifts a forkful
He imagines a piece of his thigh,
A perfect wedge of flesh.
"Stop!" he orders, taking
Her fork and beginning to eat,
Weary of their long marriage.

The siege of Sevastopol
Explodes in his dream,
His ensign's uniform is torn
Into pieces, bandages for
The wounds of his comrades.
"Let me help," he says to the man
With empty eyes, staring at
His head which has no ears.

Shouting through the darkness,
Startled by his nightmare,
The burning walls of Yasnaya Polyana
Collapsing around him,
He awakens with the image
Of his young, vibrant self
Fleeing their house in perfect order,
Leaving his books, his paintings,
Leaving everything,
Leaving his wife behind.

Turning on the bloodsown battlefield,
Both hands covering his scrotum,
He protects it from the shrapnel.
Is he awake, asleep, an officer
Or an old man with dreams
In his unruly beard?
No matter, he mounts his white mare
And gallops away.

He wants to stop his dreams,
To murder them as soon as they
Arrive, invading his nights
Like a rampaging army.
Does he want to leave his wife,
Could he kill her in a rage?
"I love her," he says, nailing his words,
Hammering them into his thoughts.

Facing his four children in the orchard,
The shadows of branches upon them,
He moves from one to the next,
His crooked fingers reaching out
To stroke their peach smooth skin.
This is the dream he never wants
To end; this, the tenderness
Missing from his grizzled old age.

Nikolai fades from one dream,
Nikolai appears in another,
Leaving tuberculosis in that French
Town as they grow old together,
Fishing at sunrise in the pond
Of never-ending childhood.
If only this dream were real,
If only he had never stood stoically
At his brother's burial.

They drank tea on the porch
Of Yasnaya Polyana, sweetened tea
Which added to the sweetness
In his dream, though Chekhov's
Persistent cough disturbed
The bluebirds in his soul
Flying toward this kindly man,
Almost his lost brother.

V

OLDEST FRIEND

I

At the Emerald Pub,
At a table in the corner
Three days after his weekly treatment
He said, "Cancer, a sneak attack,"
Clinked his glass against mine,
Cracked a dozen peanuts
With his heavy hand
Against the table
And pushed them to me.
"Go on, pretend it's
Sixty years ago."

II

Peanuts and beer,
Our pleasure at the Slop Chute.
At eighteen, determined
To become Marines,
Embracing the discipline
And challenges at Parris Island,
We sang the Hymn
Softly at dusk,
Felt our platoon molded
Into a fighting machine,
Then trained for war
At Camp Geiger—
Innocence intact.

III

On the muddy streets
Of Okinawa, leaving the Red Dragon
We spoke of Sumiko, Kimiko,
All the girls back home,
Then war games in the jungle,
The Japanese skeletons
In caves, the jumpers
On the Suicide Cliffs.
Tattooed on his forearm,
An eagle, globe, and anchor.

IV

He never looked at his
Bronze Star and Purple Heart,
He rarely spoke about
The war I missed,
His twelve month tour
In Vietnam, leading his men
Through jungles, rice paddies,
Villages; ambushes became
Routine, body counts a farce,
Agent Orange another mist.
All that mattered were his men
Coming home.

V

His crew cut, never more
Than an inch, silvered
Through the years.
A lifer, comfortable with order,
The predictable,
The pension, the retirement,
He served twenty; I, four.
We stayed in touch,
Fishing in Montana,
Remembering the past,
Embracing the present.

VI

After retirement, settling
With his family close by,
He counted cadence in his dreams,
Led his men to safety.
We lived in New England,
A different world from Vietnam,
From duty stations in the tropics.
We aged with the golden birches,
The snow melting on
The Pelham Hills.

VII

Only once did we visit
The wall, move our fingers
Over the chiseled names,
The Marines we knew.
Flowers, photographs,
Letters and crayon drawings
Rested before the wall.
No one walked away with
Their head held high.

VIII

Twenty-five push-ups began
His mornings before the cancer
As I, remembering the five-mile run
Through the steamy Parris Island dawn,
Walked slowly for the newspaper.
"The shit gets in your blood,"
He said; it was never in mine,
A short-timer waiting for discharge.
"Let's keep in touch," he said,
Steadfast in his love for the Corps.

IX

The loss of weight,
The steady drain of fatigue,
The white cells an invading army
Devouring the red
Plundered on.
He relied on morphine,
Napped through the day,
Read old issues of *Leatherneck*,
Recited his general orders.

X

We never spoke of love,
We trusted the unspoken
To lead us to places deeper
Than our words; what defined us
Were those feelings stirring within,
The acts they brought forth,
What we gave, what we received,
The ageless balance between us.

XI

His wife was stoic,
His son by her side
And I, when they left,
Remained in that white room,
Sitting quietly beside his bed.
I looked at his faded tattoo,
Placed my hand on his large one.
His eyes opened, closed,
Then opened again.
"Nothing impressive,"
Were his last words.

www.ingramcontent.com/pod-product-compliance
Lightning Source LLC
Chambersburg PA
CBHW031149090426
42738CB00008B/1268